Forgiveness Struggles?

Don Barnes

Published by Don Barnes, 2024.

LifeWorksInThrees.com

Table of Contents

About the Author

Don Barnes is the founder and author of Life Works in Threes!™ E-books. He is a lifelong Texan who has traveled extensively while taking a keen interest in human behavior. His curiosity about life and what drives humans led him to the discovery of how life works in threes. He coined this term as the *Tryune Concept*.

Don attended college on an athletic scholarship and then embarked on a 30-year career in the oil and gas industry. During his post O&G days, he got involved in a polar-bonding technology for lubrication and a liquid ozone technology used to replace chlorine for water treatment.

Along the way, he worked on his Tryune discovery, in hopes of someday sharing his findings with those struggling unnecessarily in life. What Don surmised from 40+ years of R&D was that people were struggling unnecessarily in life because they were not aware that "life works in threes." People, for the most part, are living their lives <u>by chance</u> rather than <u>by choice.</u>

From this, he began focusing on the "mechanics of life" which shows formulas for success with subjects such as *life, health, money, purpose and so forth.* When humans are able to grasp the Tryune Concept, they can apply the formula of topics that interest them and begin eliminating the struggle. This epiphany is what triggered his Tryune venture and is now on the path of sharing this amazing discovery with all who desire to improve on their lives.

Don currently resides in Southern California and Texas while overseeing his businesses and investments.

Life Works in Threes™

When I was a kid growing up, no one sat me down and said, "Okay Don, I'm going to show you how life works so that you can navigate your way through adulthood." I graduated from school, got married and went about my way with the "learn as you go" concept. It was kind of like putting together a backyard swing set without a set of instructions. Lots of frustration and do-overs, for sure!

My discovery of the "triune" word and noticing how things come together in threes is really what set me off on researching that maybe "life comes in three" ...sort of a mechanical approach to managing life, if you will. I combed the libraries and bookstores for information on this and found one book on the subject that was written back in 1951. The author's name was John S. Arant.

What Mr. Arant had to say is this "For lack of a better name, I have called this *The Triangle of Triumph* and therefore, consistent with the name, since most of these conclusions are built on the geometric figure of the triangle." He continued "All Life and all lives are seated in, and circumscribed by, the triangle. The Author and Source and Director of all life is Himself triune in character – Father, Son, and Holy Spirit. Man is of triple nature – body, mind, and spirit – and within those three there are many triangles – desires, development, decay; intellect, will, sensibilities. Of this "paced interlude in the midst of eternity" which we call time there is the triangle of Past, Present, and Future. Space – that limitless and measureless element of the physical universe – is best known in terms of Height, Breadth, and Depth. Try building yourself some triangles along the lines of your Will, your Work, your Way – You will find some interesting angles.

So, for the first time, I realized that life is designed in a mechanical way to come in threes. That means you don't have to rely on wishing and hoping things turn out okay. You can actually look at the three parts that a particular thing is made of and then apply them to get what you're wanting. Like a three-ingredient recipe or a combination lock. With a combination lock, you need the three exact numbers to unlock the lock…otherwise you will continue to struggle.

Some 40 years later, I accumulated things that work in threes and that's when I knew I needed to share this with anyone wanting answers. To have success/harmony in your life, just apply the three parts of an area you're working on, and things will fall into place. I also learned that the recipe for success with just about anything is by doing these three things, consistently – THINK positively, SPEAK positively and ACT positively. For example, if I want to be a successful artist. I would think to myself "I can do this because I have the talent." Then I would speak it this way "Yes, I am working on my art degree and plan to do portraits professionally." Finally, I would act on that by taking art classes and continue crafting my skill. Eventually, I will see the positive results/success I'm looking for.

Conversely, if I think positively but speak negatively…it will cancel out. Or if I speak positively but have no positive action going on…nothing will happen.

I looked up "How Life Works" and "The Mechanics of Life" and these are really talking about the biology of how our cells work and other chemistry. TRYUNE WORKS! teaches that life is kind of like building blocks. Pick a topic you may be struggling with. See the three parts that topic consists of and then start applying them…on a consistent basis. That will help you overcome the struggle and get you back in harmony/success with how life works.

For 30+ years I was a golf instructor (by accident). My two kids had some success playing junior golf and so friends and neighbors would ask me to show them and their kids how to play golf successfully. From all of this, I got pretty good at watching golfers on the driving range and could spot right away why they were struggling with hitting bad golf shots. I was able to do that because I knew the three steps to hitting good golf shots. I learned them from studying golf and played for several decades. I "broke the code" for me so to speak.

So now you know that life works in threes. You can live your life *by choice* rather than *by chance* and that my friend... is the key to a fulfilling life.

LIFE WORKS
IN THREES!

My sanctuary on the Pacific coast

Introduction

Forgiveness can be a bit of a tricky concept for many of us to navigate. It's like trying to untangle a mess of headphone wires — sometimes, it's clear where to start, but other times, it feels like a jumble of emotions and uncertainty. One reason for this confusion might be that forgiveness isn't a one-size-fits-all solution. It can mean different things to different people depending on their experiences and beliefs.

For some folks, forgiveness is all about letting go of anger and resentment. It's like freeing yourself from carrying around a heavy backpack full of negative feelings. But for others, forgiveness might feel more like a process rather than a single action. It could involve understanding, healing, and sometimes, it even means setting boundaries to protect yourself from getting hurt again. It's kind of like a dance — you must find your own rhythm and steps.

Another layer of confusion comes from the misconception that forgiving someone means condoning their actions. That's not necessarily the case. Forgiveness is more about releasing yourself from the grip of bitterness and moving forward with your own life. It's like saying, "Hey, what you did hurt, but I'm choosing not to let it define me anymore." It's about reclaiming your own power and peace of mind.

So, if you're feeling a bit tangled up in the idea of forgiveness, you're not alone. It's perfectly normal to have mixed feelings about it. Just remember, forgiveness isn't about forgetting or pretending everything is okay. It's about finding your own path to healing and reclaiming your inner peace.

My discovery of the Tryune Concept

Before we dive into forgiveness struggles and how to overcome them, let me share my discovery of the Tryune Concept and how life works in threes. It all began in the summer of 1982.

I grew up with parents who treated everyone with decency and respect. My three older sisters and I were raised in a home that was "middle-class traditional." We lived in modest homes in different small towns, attended school and church on a regular basis and celebrated all the traditional holidays. Eventually we settled during the spring of 1964 in the big city of Houston, Texas. I'll never forget the vastness of the city and hearing sirens from police cars, fire trucks and ambulances on a regular basis. I was excited and scared at the same time.

Once settled in this fast-paced city, I finished my growing-up years with an academic diploma and sweetheart intact. I got a job, bought a car, got married, bought a house and produced two beautiful babies in a span of about 5 years. Talk about having to grow up fast!

Things went from great in my childhood to absolute misery in my young adulthood. I began to struggle with my job because deep down I just hated what I was doing. This problem created a snowball effect because soon after, my weight, my finances, my relationships, my happiness and everything else worth saving was going down the drain. I eventually hit a level of frustration that I had never experienced before and didn't know how to get out of it. My cry for help was for anyone or anything to come to my rescue. I just ran out of solutions for my situation.

This is when my discovery happened.

One night shortly after my meltdown, while sleeping soundly, the word "triune" began to softly pound in my head like a mantra. I woke up a little startled and decided to go look up the word in my favorite dictionary (this was WAY before Google.) The definition said '**triune** (try-une) – 1) a group of three things; united. 2) Being 3 in 1 such as *humans are mental, physical and spiritual.* I scratched my head, got a glass of water and went back to bed.

The next day while driving around town, I began thinking about things that I was taught in my younger years that came in threes. My Boy Scout manual taught that to have **character**, I needed to be *1) physically strong,* 2) *mentally awake and 3) morally straight.* My high school football coach would say emphatically "If you want to be **a good football player**, you have to be *1) mobile 2) agile and 3) hostile*!" My first sales manager shared with me that to be **a successful salesman**, I needed to have *1) sales skills, 2) product knowledge and 3) a good image.*

"Hmm", I thought, "wonder if there are other examples out there of things that work in threes?" So, some 40 years later, I have researched and discovered that many, many things work in threes. What this message was telling me is that to achieve success or balance in any significant area of my life, the three things that area consisted of had to be present, continuously. That's when I had my epiphany. This discovery was telling me the secret to how life <u>really</u> works...in a mechanical way.

Tryune is a play on the word "triune" as an invitation to "try" this concept. Furthermore, we do not say that life <u>only</u> works in threes. Life also works in ones, twos, fours and so on. What has been observed though is that the many things significant to life, just so happen to come and work in threes. That's what is being shared in this book.

Now, you are about to see 40+ years of research and proof that life works in threes. I did not make up any of these topics. I invite you to research them on the internet to validate what is written here. There are some interesting facts that most of us have never realized...until now.

How Life Works in Threes (around 200 examples)

<u>LIFE</u>

Humans consist of *body, mind and soul.*

A human's basic needs are *health, income and provisions.*

A human's basic wants are *comfort, gain and approval.*

Our minds are made up of the *conscious, the subconscious and the unconscious.*

Philosophy explains *the id, the ego and superego.*

Atoms consist of *protons, neutrons and electrons.*

Motion is explained by *three basic laws.*

Science falls under three main branches: *natural, social and formal sciences*

Time is *past, present and future…*at the same time.

Electricity consists of *ohms, amperes and voltage.*

Music's basic elements are *duration, pitch and timbre.*

Democracy is a government *of the people, by the people and for the people.*

U.S. branches of government are *the judicial, the executive and the legislative.*

Armed Forces protect us on *land, air and sea.*

Environmentally, we are asked *to reduce, recycle and re-use.*

The news program gives us *the news, sports and conditions.*

Our days consist of *morning, afternoon and evening.*

Three months in each season of the year

Our main meals are known as *breakfast, lunch and dinner.*

A balanced diet consists of *good proteins, carbohydrates and fats.*

Traditional Family consists of *father, mother, and child(ren)*

<u>SCIENCES</u>

Three major branches of natural science – *(physical, earth/ space and life sciences)*

Three major branches of modern physics - *(classical, relativistic, quantum)*

Three major branches of biology *(botany, zoology, microbiology)*

Three spatial dimensions: *height* (up/down), *width* (left/ right) and *depth* (forwards/backwards)

Three-gauge bosons (photon, gluon, W&Z bosons)

Three types of elementary particles *(leptons, quarks, gauge bosons)*

Three quarks in every proton *(two "up" and one "down")*

Three primary colors of light *(red, green, blue)*

Three color tone properties *(hue, value, chroma)*

Three laws of motion (*Newton's laws*)

Three laws of planetary motion (*Kepler's laws*)

Three layers of the Sun's interior (*core, radiative zone, convective zone*)

Three layers of the Sun's atmosphere (*photosphere, chromosphere, corona*)

Three types of meteorites (*iron, stony iron, stony*)

Three types of galaxy shapes (*elliptical, spiral, irregular*)

Three substances of the universe (*normal matter, 'dark matter', 'dark energy'*)

Three phases of the moon (*new moon, first quarter, full moon*)

Three planetary regions (*temperate, sub-tropical, tropical*)

Three layers of the Earth (*crust, mantle, core*)

Three components of an ecosystem (*producers, consumers, decomposers*)

Three types of rocks (*igneous, sedimentary, metamorphic*)

Three types of fossil fuels (*coal, crude oil, natural gas*)

Three hydrological processes (*evaporation, condensation, precipitation*)

Three basic types of (meteorological) precipitation (*liquid, freezing, frozen*)

Three types of substances *(mono-constituent, multi-constituent, UVCB)*

Three phases of (normal) matter *(solid, liquid, gas)*

Three types of covalent chemical bonds *(single, double and triple bonds)*

Three isotopes of hydrogen *(protium, deuterium, tritium)*

Three atoms in each molecule of water *(two hydrogen atoms and an oxygen atom)*

Three endings to salts *(-ide, -ite, -ate)*

Three requirements for fire *(fuel, oxygen, heat)*

Three nucleotide bases in a genetic codon

Three domains of life *(archaea, bacteria and eukaryotes)*

Three major groups of flowering plants *(monocots, eudicots, magnolids)*

Three major functions that are basic to plant growth and development: *(photosynthesis* [making sugars], *respiration* [metabolizing those sugars], and *transpiration* [water vapor loss]

Three things that the chlorophyll in plants needs for photosynthesis to take place: *(sunlight, carbon dioxide and water)*

Transpiration serves three roles: *(cooling the plant, moving minerals* and *sugars through the plant,* and *maintaining the turgidity pressure* [stiffness] *of the plant's cells)*

Three parts of an insect's body *(head, thorax, abdomen)*

<u>BIOLOGY</u>

Three types of cones in the retina, relating to the three primary colors

Three semi-circular canals in the ear *(lateral, anterior, posterior)*

Three sections in the ear *(outer, middle, inner)*

Three ossicles in the middle ear *(malleus, incus, stapes)*

Three segments to each limb *(proximal, mid, distal)*

Three bones in each arm *(humerus, radius, ulna)*

Three joints in the arm *(shoulder, elbow, wrist)*

Three joints in the leg *(hip, knee, ankle)*

Three joints in the elbow *(humeroulnar, humeroradial, proximal radioulnar)*

Three functional compartments in the knee joint *(the femoropatellar, medial femorotibial* and *lateral femorotibial articulations)*

Three types of fibrous joints *(sutures, gomphoses, syndesmoses)*

Three types of bone in each hand (*carpals, metacarpals, phalanges*)

Three types of bone in each foot (*tarsals, metatarsals, phalanges*)

Three bones (phalanges) in each finger and in each toe (*proximal, intermediate, distal*)

Three layers of skin (*dermis, epidermis, hypodermis*)

Three components of a cell (*cell membrane, nucleus, cytoplasm*)

Three types of blood vessels (*arteries, veins, capillaries*)

Three types of blood cells [*red* (erythrocytes), *white* (leukocytes), *platelets* (thrombocytes)]

Three processes of the intestinal tract (*ingestion, digestion, excretion*)

Three germ layers (*Endoderm, Mesoderm, Ectoderm*)

Three parts of a human tooth (*crown, neck, root*)

Three organs of otolaryngology (*ear, nose, throat*)

Three major body systems (*digestive, circulatory, respiratory*)

Three parts to a neuron: (*soma* [*cell body*], *axon, dendrites*)

Three main parts of the brain (*forebrain, midbrain, hindbrain*)

Three parts of the forebrain *(cerebrum, thalamus, hypothalamus)*

Three parts of the midbrain *(colliculi, tegmentum, cerebral peduncles)*

Three parts of the hindbrain *(cerebellum, pons, medulla)*

Three membranes enclosing the brain *(dura mater, arachnoid, pia mater)*

The brain operates on three levels: *consciously* (for cognitive thought and declarative memory); *subconsciously* (for pre-planned actions and procedural memory); and *unconsciously* (for breathing, heart beating, etc.)

Our conscious mind is fed from three sources: *our senses* (which can be fooled); *our memory* (which is flawed); and *our imagination* (which is inventive)

Three aspects of the human mind *(memory, intellect, will)*

Three parts of the human personality *(id, ego, superego)*

The sum of human capacity consists of three abilities *(thought, word and deed)*

Three times of man *(birth, life, death)*

Three periods of the Gait Cycle *(initial double limb support, single limb support, and terminal double limb support)*

<u>MUSIC</u>

Three types of musical notes *(sharps, flats, naturals)*

Three aspects of a song (*lyrics, melody, rhythm*)

Three types of musical chords (*root, third, fifth*)

<u>MATHEMATICS</u>

Three types of a real number (*positive, negative, zero*)

Three parts to any arithmetic operation: for addition: *augend, addend and sum* - for subtraction: *minuend, subtrahend and difference* - for multiplication: *multiplicand, multiplier and product* - for division: *dividend, divisor and quotient*

Three laws of arithmetic operations (*commutative, associative, distributive*)

Three types of equivalence relation (*reflexivity, symmetry, transitivity*)

Three types of symmetry operations (*translation, rotation, reflection*)

Three geometries (*Euclidean, spherical, hyperbolic*)

The number 3 is the basis of an entire branch of mathematics, called trigonometry (from the Greek *trigonon* "triangle" + *metron* "measure")

Three trigonometric functions (*sine, cosine, tangent*)

Three types of average (*mean, mode, median*)

<u>GRAMMAR</u>

Three logical operators (*AND, OR and NOT*)

Three laws of logic (*identity, noncontradiction, excluded middle*)

Three parts of a logical syllogism (*major premise, minor premise, conclusion*)

Three grammatical parts to a sentence (*subject, verb, complement*)

Three persons in grammar [*1st person* (I/we), *2nd* (you or your), *3rd* (he/she/it/they)]

Three genders in grammar [*masculine* (he/him), *feminine* (she/her), *neuter* (it)]

Three forms of comparison in grammar [*positive, comparative* (more, -er), *superlative* (most, -est)]

Three cases in (English) grammar [*subjective/nominative* (he), *objective/accusative* (him) and *possessive/genitive* (his)]

Three parts of a narrative (*beginning, middle, end*)

Components of an essay (*introduction, body, conclusion*)

Elements of a rhetorical appeal (*ethos, pathos, logos*)

Aspects of a story (*plot, characters, setting*)

<u>RELIGION</u>

The Creator – *omniscient, omnipotent, omnipresent*

Christian God – *Father, Son, Holy Spirit*

Jesus – *The Way, The Truth, The Life*

Ancient Near East- *Qudshu, Astarte, Anat*

Classical Antiquity – Many dieties came in threes

Hinduism – Para Brahman is *Brahma, Visnu, Shiva*

Ancient Celtic Cultures – *many example of triad dieties*

Buddhism – *The three jewels*

Taoism – *The three pure ones*

Islam – *Fear, Hope and Love*

Baha'i - *Intention, Power and Action*

Confucianism – *Benevolence, Wisdom and Courage*

<u>OTHER TRIUNE EXAMPLES</u>

3 Coins in a Fountain

3 Days of the Condor

3 Miles in a League

3 Goals in a Hat Trick

3 Piece Suit

3 Feet in a Yard

3 Books in Lord of the Rings

3 Ring Circus

3 Ships of Christopher Columbus

3 Sheets to the Wind

3 Books in a Trilogy

3 Wheels on a Tricycle

3 Wise Men

3-Legged Race

3 Ring Circus

3-Wheeler

3 Cornered Hat

3 Dimensional

3 Musketeers

3 R's (reading, 'riting, 'rithmatic)

3 Sides of a triangle

3 Races in the Triple Crown (horse racing)

3 Angles in a Triangle

3 Trimesters in a Pregnancy

3 Flavors in Neapolitan Ice Cream

3 Stars in Orion's belt

3 Barleycorns in an Inch

3 Hands on a Clock (with the Seconds Hand)

3 Colors in a Flag

3 Minute Egg

3 Great Pyramids at Giza

3 Holes in a Bowling Ball

3 Colors in a Set of Traffic Lights

3 Minutes in a Boxing Round

3 Teaspoons in a Tablespoon

3 Legs on a Stool

3 Monastic Vows (Obience, Stability, Conversatio Morum)

3 Body Types: Endomorph, Mesomorph, Ectomorph

3 Ring Notebooks

3 Germ layers: Endoderm, Mesoderm, Ectoderm

3 Species of Homo: Homo habilis, Homo erectus, Homo sapiens

3 Basic parts of a camera: Lens, Shutter, Sensor

3 Stages of a Project lifecycle: initiation, planning, execution

The Truth, The Whole Truth and Nothing but the Truth

Life, Liberty and the Pursuit of Happiness

Hear no Evil, See no Evil, Speak no Evil

National motto of France/Haiti: Liberty, Equality, Fraternity

Paper, Rock, Scissors

Ready, Aim, Fire

On Your mark, Get Set, Go

Olympic medals of gold, silver, bronze

Types of joints (ball & socket, hinge, pivot)

Stages of a rocket launch (launch, orbit, re-entry)

Parts of a joke (setup, delivery, punchline)

Primary components of a transistor (emitter, base, collector)

Primary components of an airplane (fuselage, wings, empennage)

Basic components of a computer: CPU, memory, storage

Three phases in the development of technology (*eotechnic* [*mechanical*], *paleotechnic* [*steam-powered*] and *neotechnic* [*electric-powered*]

Communication systems require three components (*transmitter, channel, receiver*)

The list goes on. See if you can find more examples as they are everywhere in our universe. Now that you know that life works in threes (with proof!), we can begin to apply this concept to whatever topics we want.

So, to overcome struggles with forgiveness, we need to apply the three areas that forgiveness consists of – WHY, WHEN and HOW. Let's get started!

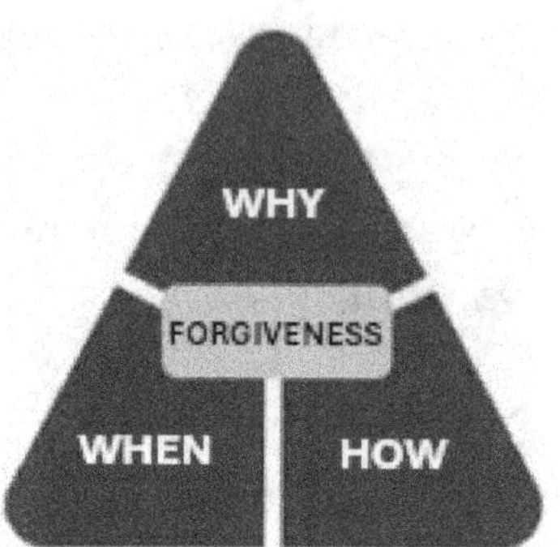
WHY
FORGIVENESS
WHEN
HOW

FORGIVENESS

Considering forgiveness can be a profound act of self-care and emotional maturity. It's like giving yourself permission to heal and move forward rather than staying stuck in a cycle of resentment and pain. One important reason to consider forgiving a person or situation is that it allows you to reclaim your own peace of mind. Holding onto grudges is like carrying around a heavy weight that drags you down. When you entertain the idea of forgiveness, it's like starting to unload that weight, bit by bit, until you feel lighter and more at ease.

Another compelling reason to consider forgiveness is that it can foster personal growth and resilience. It's like turning a stumbling block into a steppingstone. When you choose to forgive, you're not just letting go of negative feelings; you're also embracing the opportunity to learn from your experiences and become stronger. It's a chance to reflect on what you've learned, how you've grown, and how you can approach similar situations in the future with more wisdom and grace.

Moreover, considering forgiveness can be a powerful act of compassion, both towards yourself and others involved. It's like extending an olive branch in a garden of misunderstandings. Forgiveness doesn't always mean forgetting or excusing someone's actions; rather, it's about acknowledging humanity in yourself and others. It allows you to see beyond the hurt and recognize that everyone makes mistakes or faces challenges. By considering forgiveness, you're opening the door to empathy and understanding, which can pave the way for deeper connections and more harmonious relationships in the long run. Ultimately, forgiveness is a gift you give yourself — a gift of inner peace, growth, and compassionate living.

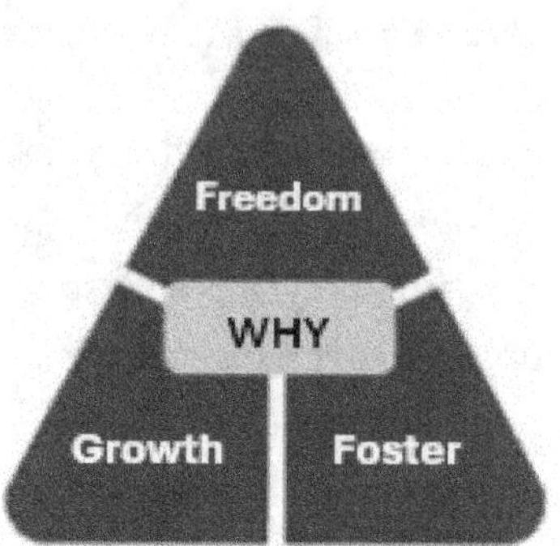
Freedom
WHY
Growth
Foster

WHY

Forgiving someone or a situation can be incredibly beneficial. Here are three reasons why it's worth considering:

1. **Emotional Freedom**: Forgiveness liberates you from carrying the burden of anger, resentment, or bitterness. When you forgive, you release negative emotions that can weigh you down, allowing you to experience greater peace of mind and emotional well-being.

2. **Personal Growth**: Forgiveness is a powerful catalyst for personal growth. It encourages introspection and empathy, helping you understand others' perspectives and your own reactions better. It fosters resilience and strengthens your ability to handle conflicts constructively.

3. **Improved Relationships**: Forgiveness can mend relationships and promote reconciliation. By letting go of grudges or past hurts, you create space for healthier interactions and deeper connections with others. It fosters trust, mutual respect, and a more positive environment for both parties involved.

Ultimately, forgiveness is a gift you give yourself, offering the opportunity to move forward with a lighter heart and a more positive outlook on life.

There is nothing that says you must forgive someone or something, but experience reveals that over time it will start to eat at you. As stated before, forgiveness does not mean that we are okay with what happened or condoning it. It's really allowing yourself to "keep the lesson and throw away the experience" so you can get on with your life. At the very least, you can "consider" forgiving someone or something and that's a start. Just consider it and if and when you feel like it... move on to the next step.

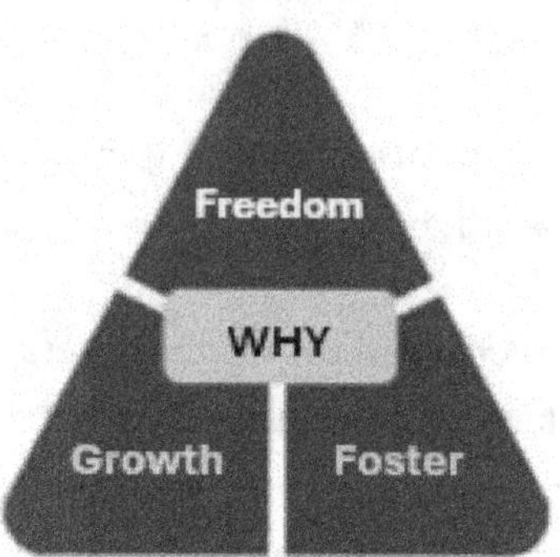
Freedom
WHY
Growth
Foster

Freedom

When someone chooses to forgive, they embark on a transformative journey towards emotional freedom. Forgiveness isn't just about letting go of past grievances; it's about reclaiming inner peace and serenity. By releasing the grip of anger and resentment, individuals open themselves to a profound sense of relief. It's like lifting a weight off their shoulders, allowing them to breathe easier and think clearer. This emotional liberation enables them to focus their energy on positive aspects of life rather than dwelling on negativity. It's a powerful act of self-care and self-empowerment, demonstrating strength in choosing peace over conflict.

Moreover, forgiveness cultivates resilience and emotional strength. It requires courage to confront painful experiences and consciously decide to move forward without bitterness. This process of healing fosters personal growth and maturity. It encourages individuals to learn from their experiences, gain perspective, and develop empathy. By forgiving, people often discover newfound empathy for themselves and others, understanding that everyone is flawed and capable of mistakes. This empathy builds bridges rather than walls, creating deeper connections and fostering healthier relationships.

In addition to personal growth, forgiveness contributes to overall well-being and mental health. It reduces stress, anxiety, and negative emotions that can otherwise consume a person's thoughts and actions. Instead, forgiveness promotes a sense of inner harmony and emotional stability. It allows individuals to cultivate a positive outlook on life, finding joy in everyday moments and embracing a hopeful future. Ultimately, the emotional freedom found in forgiveness isn't just a gift to oneself; it radiates outward, positively impacting relationships and creating a more compassionate and understanding community.

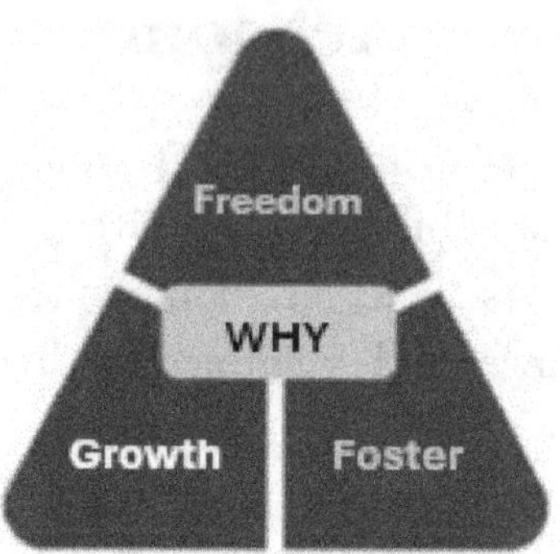

Freedom
WHY
Growth
Foster

Growth

Forgiveness is a profound catalyst for personal growth, empowering individuals to transcend past hurts and evolve into stronger, more resilient versions of themselves. When someone chooses to forgive, they embark on a journey of introspection and self-discovery. They confront their own vulnerabilities and confrontations, gaining insights into their values and beliefs. This process fosters a deeper understanding of their emotional triggers and responses, enabling them to cultivate greater emotional intelligence and self-awareness.

Moreover, forgiveness nurtures empathy and compassion. By forgiving, individuals acknowledge the humanity in both themselves and others, recognizing that everyone makes mistakes and deserves understanding. This empathy strengthens interpersonal relationships, fostering trust and mutual respect. It encourages open communication and conflict resolution skills, empowering individuals to navigate future challenges with grace and maturity.

Furthermore, forgiveness cultivates resilience in the face of adversity. It teaches individuals to adapt and grow from setbacks, rather than being consumed by bitterness or resentment. This resilience is essential for navigating life's complexities and uncertainties, enabling individuals to bounce back stronger after experiencing pain or betrayal. By embracing forgiveness, individuals not only heal from past wounds but also empower themselves to embrace new opportunities and experiences with an open heart and mind.

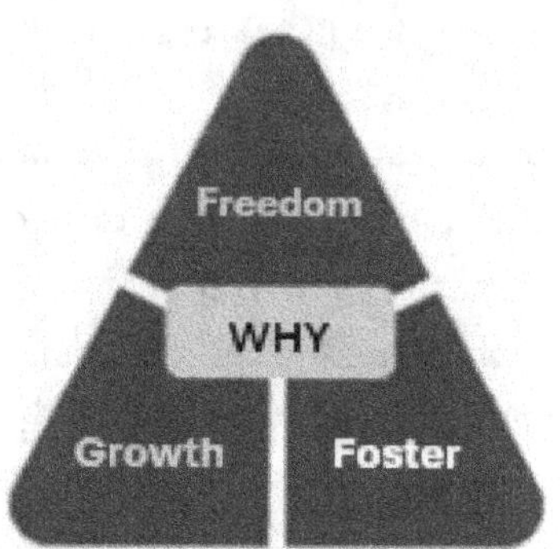

Freedom
WHY
Growth
Foster

Foster

Forgiveness is a powerful tool for building and maintaining trust in relationships. When someone chooses to forgive, they demonstrate a willingness to let go of past grievances and move forward with an open heart. This act of compassion and understanding reassures others that they can be vulnerable and make mistakes without fear of permanent judgment or rejection. It creates a safe space for open communication and honest dialogue, essential ingredients for fostering deep and meaningful connections.

Moreover, forgiveness cultivates empathy and understanding. By forgiving others, individuals acknowledge that everyone is imperfect and capable of missteps. This realization promotes a sense of mutual respect and compassion, strengthening the bonds of empathy between individuals. It encourages a culture of forgiveness and acceptance within relationships, where both parties feel valued and understood, even amidst disagreements or conflicts.

Furthermore, forgiveness paves the way for reconciliation and healing. It allows relationships to transcend past hurts and grievances, enabling individuals to rebuild trust and repair damaged connections. This process is transformative, as it encourages individuals to focus on the positive aspects of their relationships and envision a future built on mutual respect and support. By fostering forgiveness, individuals create a foundation of trust and empathy that sustains healthy relationships over time, promoting harmony and cooperation in both personal and professional spheres.

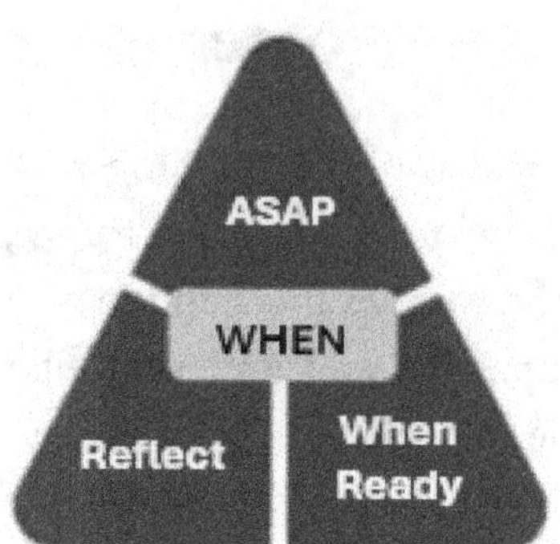
ASAP
WHEN
Reflect
When
Ready

WHEN

Now that you are in a frame of mind to consider forgiveness, when is a good time to do that? Here are some suggestions:

1. **Soon After the Incident**: It's often beneficial to consider forgiveness relatively soon after an incident or conflict. Emotions are still fresh, and addressing the issue promptly can prevent negative feelings from festering and potentially damaging the relationship further. By forgiving early on, individuals demonstrate maturity and a willingness to prioritize resolution over resentment, fostering a quicker path to healing and reconciliation.

2. **After Reflecting on the Situation**: Taking time to reflect on the situation can provide valuable perspective before extending forgiveness. This timeframe allows individuals to process their emotions, understand their own reactions, and consider the circumstances from various angles. It's important to approach forgiveness from a place of clarity and understanding rather than impulsiveness or pressure. Reflective forgiveness promotes personal growth and enhances the sincerity of the forgiveness gesture, contributing to stronger relationships built on empathy and mutual respect.

3. **When Ready to Let Go of Resentment**: Forgiveness should be considered when individuals are ready to let go of resentment and negative emotions associated with the incident. Holding onto grudges can be emotionally taxing and detrimental to personal well-being. When individuals feel ready to release the burden of anger or hurt, forgiveness becomes a liberating choice that promotes emotional freedom and inner peace. This readiness indicates a commitment to prioritizing the relationship's health and moving forward with

a positive outlook.

In each of these timeframes, approaching forgiveness in a friendly and understanding tone fosters openness and communication, paving the way for deeper understanding and stronger connections with others. It's a process that requires introspection, empathy, and a genuine desire for reconciliation and personal growth.

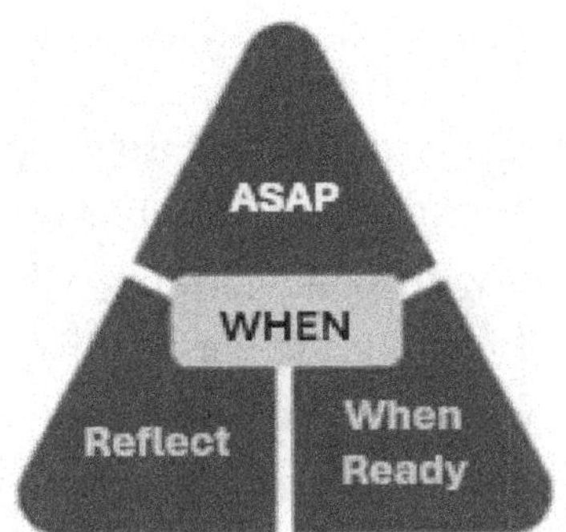
ASAP
WHEN
Reflect
When
Ready

ASAP

Forgiveness is like a magic potion for the soul—it lightens your burden and frees your spirit. When we forgive quickly, we reclaim our peace of mind almost instantly. Imagine carrying a heavy backpack full of resentment and hurt; forgiving someone is like setting that backpack down and feeling the weight lift off your shoulders. It's not just about letting go of the past but also about opening up space for positivity and growth in your life.

One of the sweetest advantages of forgiving promptly is that it prevents negativity from taking root and spreading. Holding onto grudges can poison our thoughts and interactions, affecting not only our mental well-being but also our relationships with others. By forgiving swiftly, we stop the cycle of negativity in its tracks and pave the way for healthier, happier connections. It's like hitting the refresh button on a strained friendship or a tense situation—suddenly, there's room for understanding and reconciliation.

Moreover, forgiving early on fosters resilience and inner strength. It shows that you have the courage to rise above hurt feelings and take control of your emotional state. Instead of dwelling on what went wrong, you focus on how to move forward constructively. This resilience not only benefits your personal growth but also inspires those around you. It's a powerful reminder that forgiveness isn't a sign of weakness but rather a testament to your maturity and ability to navigate life's challenges with grace.

In essence, forgiving as soon as possible isn't just about letting someone off the hook—it's about setting yourself free from the chains of resentment, cultivating healthier relationships, and fortifying your own inner strength. So, the next time you find yourself grappling with hurt or anger, consider the liberating power of forgiveness. Your future self will thank you for it!

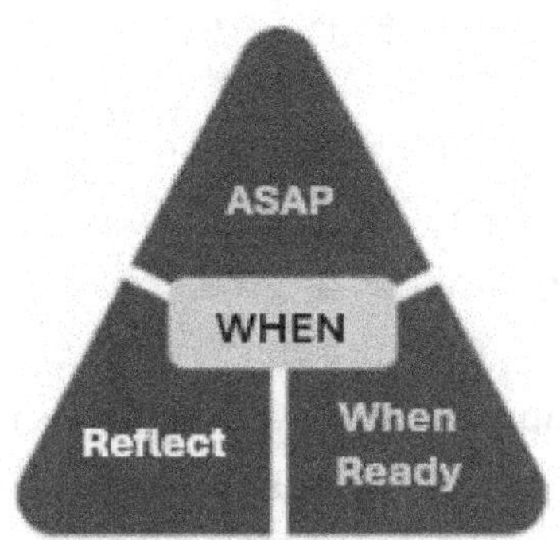

ASAP
WHEN
Reflect
When
Ready

Reflect

Reflecting on forgiveness with someone or something can be a profound journey of self-discovery and healing. When we take the time to explore our feelings and thoughts about forgiveness, especially with others who may have insights or shared experiences, it opens up avenues for deeper understanding and empathy. Sharing this process in a friendly and open tone not only strengthens relationships but also fosters a supportive environment where healing can flourish.

Discussing forgiveness with someone allows us to gain new perspectives and insights that we might not have considered on our own. It invites us to see situations from different angles, which can be incredibly enlightening. Sometimes, simply talking about our feelings with a trusted friend or counselor can help us unravel complex emotions and find clarity in our decision-making process regarding forgiveness.

Moreover, reflecting on forgiveness with others reinforces the idea that forgiveness is a multifaceted journey rather than a one-time event. It acknowledges the complexities of human relationships and emotions, emphasizing that forgiveness is not always straightforward but requires patience, empathy, and self-reflection. By engaging in these conversations in a friendly and supportive manner, we create spaces where vulnerability is embraced, and healing can take place organically.

In essence, reflecting on forgiveness with someone or something offers us an opportunity to deepen our emotional intelligence and strengthen our bonds with others. It's a collaborative process that honors our shared humanity and promotes growth on both individual and relational levels. So, next time you find yourself grappling with forgiveness, consider reaching out to someone you trust to embark on this meaningful journey together.

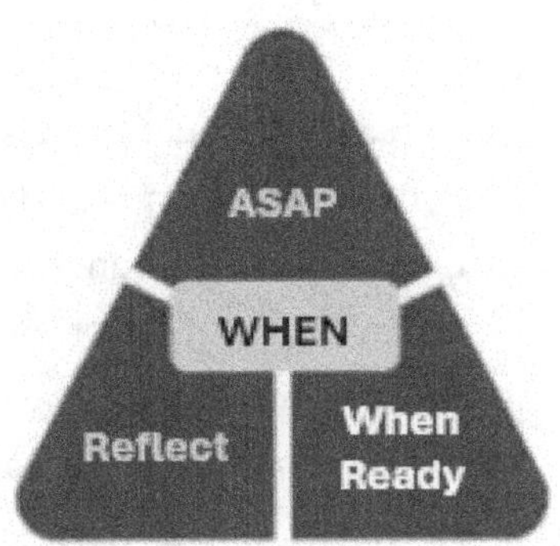

ASAP
WHEN
Reflect
When
Ready

When Ready

Forgiving when you're truly ready is a deeply personal and empowering choice. It's about honoring your own journey and emotions, recognizing that healing takes time and patience. When you forgive at your own pace, you ensure that it's a genuine and heartfelt decision, rather than something forced or rushed. This readiness allows you to fully embrace the healing process and move forward with a sense of peace and authenticity.

Choosing to forgive when you feel ready also signifies a profound sense of self-awareness and emotional maturity. It shows that you've taken the time to process your feelings, understand the situation from different perspectives, and come to terms with the impact it has had on you. This readiness isn't about forgetting or condoning what happened but rather about releasing the hold it has on your heart and mind.

Moreover, forgiving when you're ready empowers you to set boundaries and prioritize your own well-being. It's a declaration of self-respect and self-care, affirming that you deserve to live without the weight of resentment or bitterness. By allowing yourself the time and space to forgive on your terms, you reclaim your emotional autonomy and pave the way for personal growth and positive change.

In essence, forgiving when you're ready is a gentle yet powerful act of kindness toward yourself. It's a reminder that healing is a gradual process that unfolds at its own pace. So, trust your instincts, listen to your heart, and when the time feels right, embrace forgiveness as a gift you give yourself. Your readiness will guide you toward a brighter, more peaceful future.

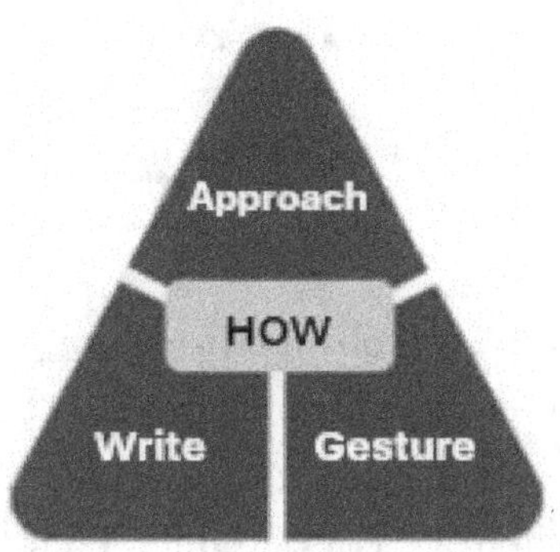

Approach
HOW
Write
Gesture

HOW

Here are three ways to offer forgiveness to someone who has offended you:

1. **Open and Honest Conversation**: <u>Approach the person</u> in a calm and non-confrontational manner. Express how their actions or words affected you, using "I" statements to avoid sounding accusatory. For example, "I felt hurt when..." or "I was upset because...". Listen to their perspective as well and try to understand their intentions. This open dialogue can lead to mutual understanding and pave the way for forgiveness.

1. **Write a Thoughtful Letter**: If a face-to-face conversation feels daunting or if the person is not physically present, <u>consider writing a letter</u>. Choose your words carefully to convey your feelings and your decision to forgive. Be compassionate and understanding in your tone, emphasizing your desire to move forward positively. This method allows you to articulate your thoughts clearly and gives the recipient time to reflect without immediate pressure.

1. **Symbolic Gesture or Act of Kindness**: Sometimes, forgiveness can be communicated through actions rather than words. Consider <u>offering a symbolic gesture</u>, such as inviting the person to coffee or sending a small gift or card. This gesture should be sincere and without expectation of reciprocity. It shows that you are willing to let go of resentment and rebuild a positive connection. This approach can be especially effective in restoring harmony and fostering a renewed sense of trust.

Approaching forgiveness in a friendly manner not only heals wounds but also strengthens relationships by promoting empathy and understanding. It allows both parties to grow emotionally and move forward with greater peace of mind.

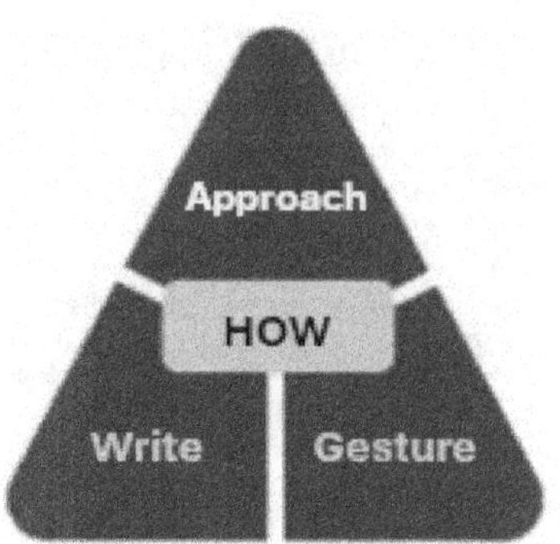
Approach
HOW
Write
Gesture

Approach

Approaching someone about forgiveness in a friendly tone can yield numerous benefits, both for yourself and for the relationship involved. Firstly, a friendly approach creates a conducive atmosphere for open communication and understanding. When you initiate the conversation with kindness and empathy, you set a tone that encourages the other person to listen and respond positively. This can lead to a more productive dialogue where both parties feel safe expressing their thoughts and emotions without fear of judgment or hostility.

Secondly, a friendly approach to forgiveness fosters emotional healing and growth. By choosing to forgive in a warm and respectful manner, you release negative emotions such as anger, resentment, and bitterness. This act of letting go can be incredibly liberating, allowing you to move forward with a lighter heart and a clearer mind. It also promotes personal development by cultivating qualities such as patience, empathy, and forgiveness within yourself.

Lastly, approaching forgiveness in a friendly tone strengthens relationships and builds trust. When someone feels genuinely forgiven and understood, they are more likely to reciprocate with gratitude and a desire to mend any rifts. This process can deepen your bond with the other person, as it demonstrates your commitment to resolving conflicts and nurturing a healthy connection. Ultimately, by choosing a friendly approach to forgiveness, you contribute to a more harmonious and supportive environment where mutual respect and understanding thrive.

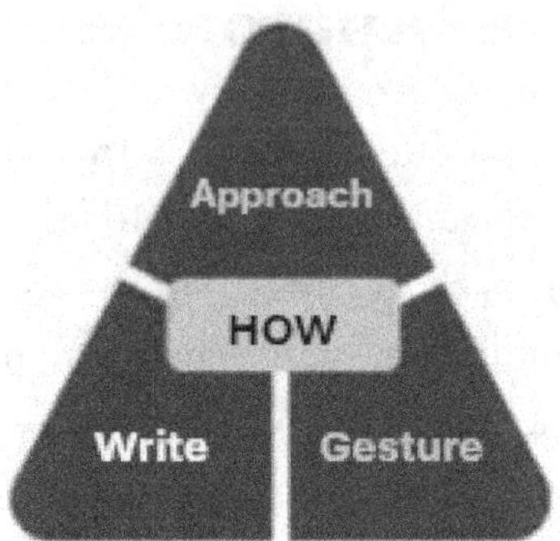
Approach
HOW
Write
Gesture

Write

Writing a letter to someone about forgiveness in a friendly tone offers several distinct advantages that can facilitate healing and reconciliation. Firstly, a letter provides a structured and thoughtful means of expressing your emotions and thoughts without the immediate pressure of a face-to-face conversation. This can be particularly beneficial if you find it challenging to articulate your feelings verbally or if the person is not physically present. You can carefully choose your words, ensuring they convey your sincerity, empathy, and desire for reconciliation.

Secondly, a written letter allows the recipient to process your message at their own pace. Unlike a conversation where responses can be immediate and potentially reactive, a letter gives the person time to reflect calmly on what you've expressed. This can lead to a more thoughtful and considered response, fostering a deeper understanding of each other's perspectives and feelings. It also reduces the likelihood of misunderstandings that can arise in verbal communication.

Lastly, writing a letter about forgiveness in a friendly tone can serve as a tangible symbol of your willingness to forgive and move forward positively. It demonstrates your commitment to resolving conflicts with empathy and respect, regardless of the outcome. This act of reaching out can plant the seeds for rebuilding trust and strengthening the relationship over time. Even if the letter doesn't lead to immediate reconciliation, it can still contribute to your own emotional healing and personal growth by allowing you to release negative emotions and cultivate a sense of inner peace.

In summary, writing a letter about forgiveness in a friendly tone provides a structured, reflective, and sincere approach to resolving conflicts and nurturing relationships. It offers both practical and emotional benefits, ultimately promoting healing, understanding, and the potential for renewed harmony in your interactions with others.

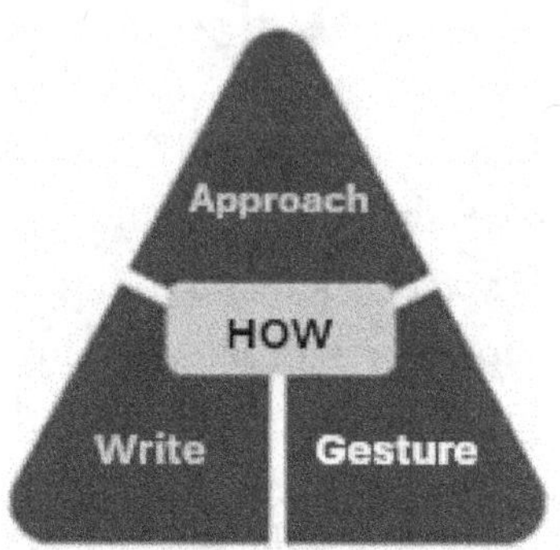
Approach
HOW
Write
Gesture

Gesture

Offering a symbolic gesture to show forgiveness towards someone in a friendly tone can be incredibly impactful and beneficial for both parties involved. Firstly, such gestures serve as tangible expressions of your willingness to let go of grievances and move forward positively. Whether it's a small gift, a kind gesture, or an invitation to spend time together, these acts convey sincerity and empathy, signaling to the other person that you value the relationship and are committed to repairing any rifts that may exist.

Secondly, a symbolic gesture can help to bridge the gap of understanding between you and the other person. It provides an opportunity to communicate non-verbally, often transcending words and allowing emotions to be expressed more intuitively. This can be particularly effective in situations where verbal communication may be difficult or strained. The gesture itself can speak volumes about your intentions and feelings, fostering a sense of connection and mutual respect.

Lastly, offering a symbolic gesture of forgiveness in a friendly tone promotes healing and emotional well-being. It can alleviate feelings of guilt or remorse within yourself while also offering the other person a chance to experience relief and closure. Such gestures create a positive atmosphere conducive to reconciliation and rebuilding trust. They pave the way for renewed harmony in the relationship, encouraging both parties to focus on moving forward with understanding and empathy.

In essence, symbolic gestures of forgiveness in a friendly tone not only communicate your desire for reconciliation but also facilitate healing and strengthen bonds. They embody the principles of empathy and kindness, contributing to a healthier and more supportive relationship dynamic over time.

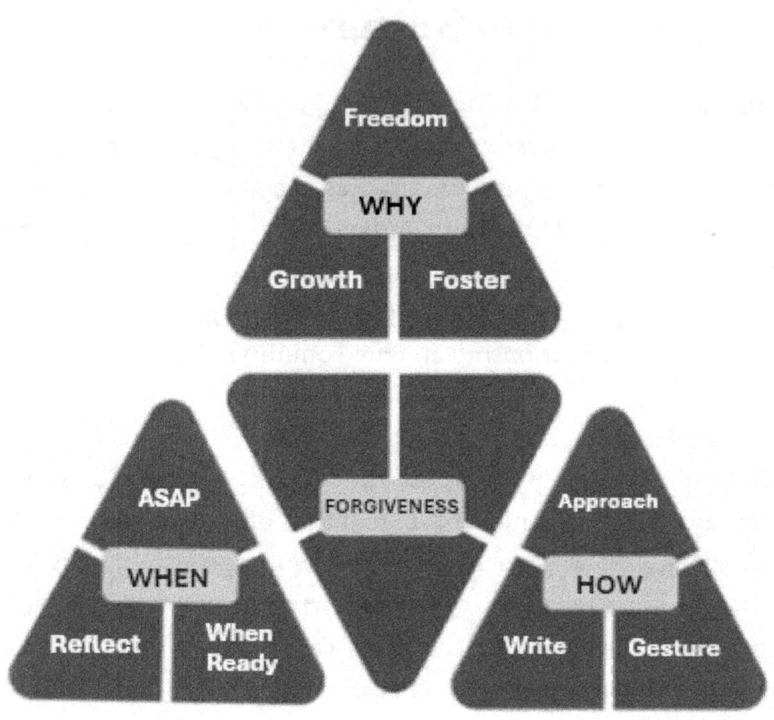

Freedom
WHY
Growth
Foster
ASAP
WHEN
Reflect
When Ready
FORGIVENESS
Approach
HOW
Write
Gesture

SUMMARY

The saying "what doesn't kill you makes you stronger" holds a profound truth that resonates with many of life's challenges. It suggests that difficult experiences, though painful and trying, can ultimately lead to personal growth and resilience. This sentiment encourages us to see adversity as a potential source of strength rather than a setback. It invites us to embrace challenges with optimism, knowing that each hurdle we overcome contributes to our inner fortitude and character development.

When we encounter setbacks or hardships, it's natural to feel disheartened or discouraged. However, approaching these situations with a positive perspective allows us to shift our focus towards the lessons they offer. Every trial presents an opportunity for learning and self-discovery. By navigating through tough times with patience and determination, we not only survive but also gain valuable insights and skills that prepare us for future obstacles.

The concept of resilience is deeply rooted in our ability to adapt and bounce back from adversity. Each time we confront and overcome difficulties, we build emotional strength and mental toughness. This resilience enables us to face future challenges with greater confidence and clarity. It teaches us to trust in our own capabilities and to find silver linings even in the darkest of times. Ultimately, adopting a healthy outlook towards the idea that "what doesn't kill you makes you stronger" empowers us to embrace life's ups and downs as essential parts of our personal growth journey.

When you're with someone who is sharing their struggles with you...just smile at him/her and give them one of these. He/she will ask "What is that?" Then simply reply "Life Works in Threes."

Invitation

In life, we sometimes encounter situations or actions that seem unforgivable. These can be deeply personal betrayals, severe injustices, or traumas that leave lasting scars on our hearts and minds. It's natural to feel conflicted and torn when faced with such circumstances, as forgiveness may seem impossible or undeserved. However, amidst the weight of these grievances, there is a profound truth: <u>life must go on</u>. This realization is not about condoning or forgetting the wrongs done to us but about acknowledging that dwelling on unforgivable acts can hinder our ability to live fully in the present and find peace within ourselves.

Accepting that some things are unforgivable doesn't mean we allow bitterness or resentment to consume us. Instead, it encourages us to focus on healing and self-preservation. It's about reclaiming our sense of agency and refusing to let past hurts define our future. By prioritizing our well-being and emotional health, we empower ourselves to move forward with strength and resilience.

Moreover, recognizing the reality that some actions are beyond forgiveness underscores the importance of boundaries and self-care. It's okay to protect ourselves from further harm and to distance us from toxic or harmful situations. This self-preservation isn't a sign of weakness but a testament to our innate instinct for survival and personal growth. Life's journey is about navigating the complexities of human relationships and experiences, and sometimes, part of that journey involves accepting that *while forgiveness may not be possible, our own journey must continue.*

I invite you to consider the possibility that while we may not be able to forgive someone or something on a severe magnitude... we still must pick up the pieces and get on with our lives. Otherwise, we begin to rot from the inside out – and that's not a good thing.

Living in the real world

Living in a world that is imperfect and chaotic presents a myriad of challenges that affect individuals, communities, and societies at large. At its core, the unpredictability and imperfections inherent in our surroundings can induce feelings of uncertainty and instability. Individuals often find themselves grappling with constant change, whether it's economic fluctuations, political unrest, natural disasters, or personal crises. This perpetual state of flux can erode a sense of security and control, leaving people vulnerable and anxious about the future.

Moreover, the imperfections within societal structures amplify disparities and injustices. Economic inequalities, systemic discrimination, and geopolitical tensions create barriers that hinder progress and perpetuate cycles of disadvantage. These issues not only strain relationships between individuals and communities but also challenge collective efforts to foster cohesion and unity. The resulting societal friction often leads to polarization and conflict, further complicating efforts to achieve harmony and cooperation.

Psychologically, living in such a world can take a toll on mental health. The constant bombardment of negative news, coupled with personal struggles and societal pressures, can breed feelings of helplessness, hopelessness, and despair. Individuals may struggle to find meaning and purpose amidst the chaos, questioning their own agency and capacity to effect meaningful change.

Furthermore, the imperfections and chaos of the world can test moral and ethical boundaries. Individuals may face dilemmas where difficult choices must be made between personal gain and the greater good, or between short-term benefits and long-term sustainability. Navigating these ethical gray areas can be daunting, as moral compasses are challenged by conflicting priorities and perspectives.

Despite these challenges, living in an imperfect and chaotic world also offers opportunities for growth, resilience, and solidarity. Individuals and communities often demonstrate remarkable adaptability and creativity in responding to adversity. Acts of kindness, courage, and collaboration emerge as beacons of hope amidst the turmoil, showcasing the innate human capacity for compassion and innovation.

In essence, while the challenges of living in an imperfect and chaotic world are profound and multifaceted, they also underscore the resilience and potential for positive transformation within individuals and societies. Embracing this complexity requires acknowledging the imperfections while striving towards greater understanding, empathy, and collective action to build a more just and sustainable future.

Some things are just not forgivable

Here are some examples of actions or behaviors that many people consider unforgivable:

1. **Intentional Murder**: Taking someone's life with malicious intent.
2. **Terrorism**: Acts of violence and destruction aimed at causing fear and harm to civilians.
3. **Sexual Abuse or Assault**: Violating another person's bodily autonomy and dignity.
4. **Genocide**: Deliberate and systematic extermination of a national, racial, political, or cultural group.
5. **Betrayal of Trust**: Severe breaches of trust such as infidelity in a committed relationship or betraying confidential information.
6. **Child Abuse**: Physical, emotional, or sexual mistreatment of children.
7. **Torture**: Inflicting severe physical or psychological pain on someone intentionally.
8. **Human Trafficking**: Exploiting individuals through forced labor or sexual exploitation.
9. **Extreme Racism or Hate Crimes**: Committing acts motivated by intense racial, ethnic, or religious prejudice.
10. **Causing Irreparable Harm**: Actions that result in permanent physical or psychological damage to others.

Forgiveness can be a complex and deeply personal process, influenced by various factors including cultural norms, religious beliefs, and individual values. While some people might find it within themselves to forgive certain actions under specific circumstances, others may consider these actions fundamentally unforgivable.

So, what do we then? Call the law, then wash your hands of it.

"I will remember and recover, not forgive and forget."

Other titles coming out:

- Weight Struggles?
- Abundance Struggles?
- Parenting Struggles?
- Life Struggles?
- Purpose Struggles?
- Happiness Struggles?
- Sales Struggles?
- Speaker Struggles?
- Time Struggles?
- Network Struggles?
- Marriage Struggles?
- Divorce Struggles?
- Money Struggles?
- Career Struggles?
- Dating Struggles?
- Caretaker Struggles?
- Romance Struggles?
- Grieving Struggles?
- Success Struggles?
- Golf Struggles?
- Workplace Struggles?
- Stress Struggles?
- Shame/Guilt Struggles?
- Addiction Struggles?

Remember,
When you get right down to it,

Life is about making choices.

Every day, all day long, that's what we do.

- *We choose to get out of bed or not.*
- *We choose to clean up or not.*
- *We choose what to eat all day.*
- *We choose to exercise or not.*
- *We choose to go to work or not.*
- *We choose to do a good job or not.*
- *We choose to come home or not.*
- *We choose to watch TV or do something constructive.*
- *We choose to bed at a decent hour or not.*

And the next day…we start all over again.

What is the meaning of this? Get good at choosing.

Before you can get good at choosing though…you need to understand how life works in threes.

Courtesy of SymbolSage.com

When someone is struggling with a particular area or two, chances are they are "out of balance" with how life works. How does life work? Life works in threes.

If you're interested in personal topics like life, health, money or business topics like sales, time management and public speaking...TRYUNE WORKS! can shed some light on creating success in those areas.

The definition of TRIUNE is a group of three things; united. Being three in one, such as - humans are *mental, physical* and *spiritual beings*. The word TRYUNE is a play of the word TRIUNE, encouraging all to try this concept and help eliminate struggling unnecessarily.

LifeWorksInThrees.com

www.ingramcontent.com/pod-product-compliance
Lightning Source LLC
Chambersburg PA
CBHW061358140726
47997CB00003B/1268